Spiders

Experts on child reading levels
have consulted on the level of text and
concepts in this book.

At the end of the book is a "Look Back and Find" section
which provides additional information and encourages
the child to refer back to previous pages
for the answers to the questions posed.

Angela Grunsell trained as a teacher in 1969.
She has a Diploma in Reading and Related Skills
and for the last five years has advised London
teachers on materials and resources.
She worked for the ILEA as an
advisory teacher and is currently
teaching in a primary school in Hackney, London.

Published in Great Britain in 1985
Franklin Watts, 12a Golden Square, London W1

Designed and produced by
Aladdin Books Ltd, 70 Old Compton Street, London W1

ISBN 0 86313 327 4

Printed in Belgium

FRANKLIN · WATTS · FIRST · LIBRARY

Spiders

by
Kate Petty

Consultant
Angela Grunsell

Illustrated by
Alan Baker

Franklin Watts
London · New York · Toronto · Sydney

Have you noticed that spiders have eight legs?
Usually they have eight eyes too.
A spider is an "arachnid" and not an insect.
Insects have only six legs.

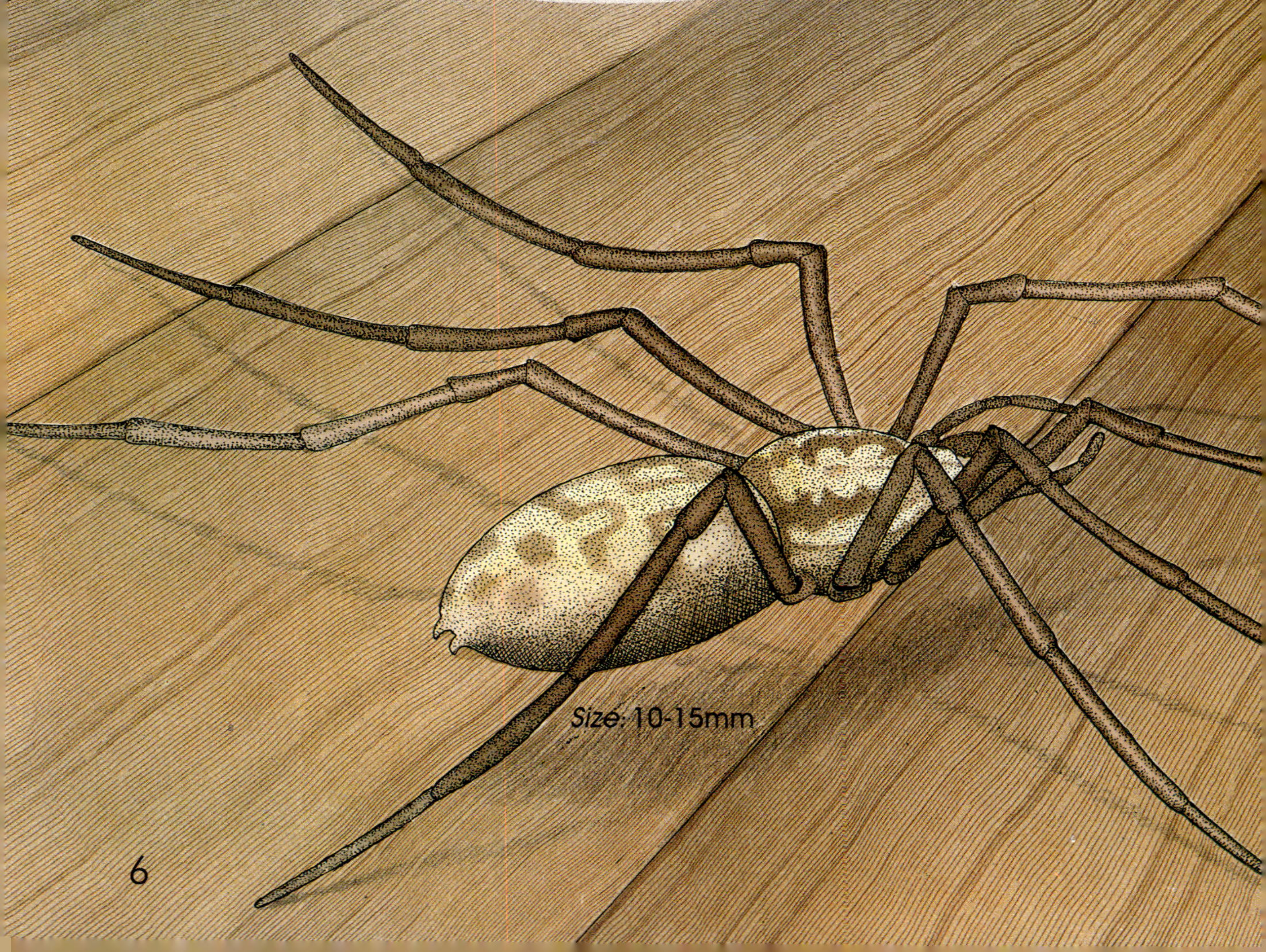

Size: 10-15mm

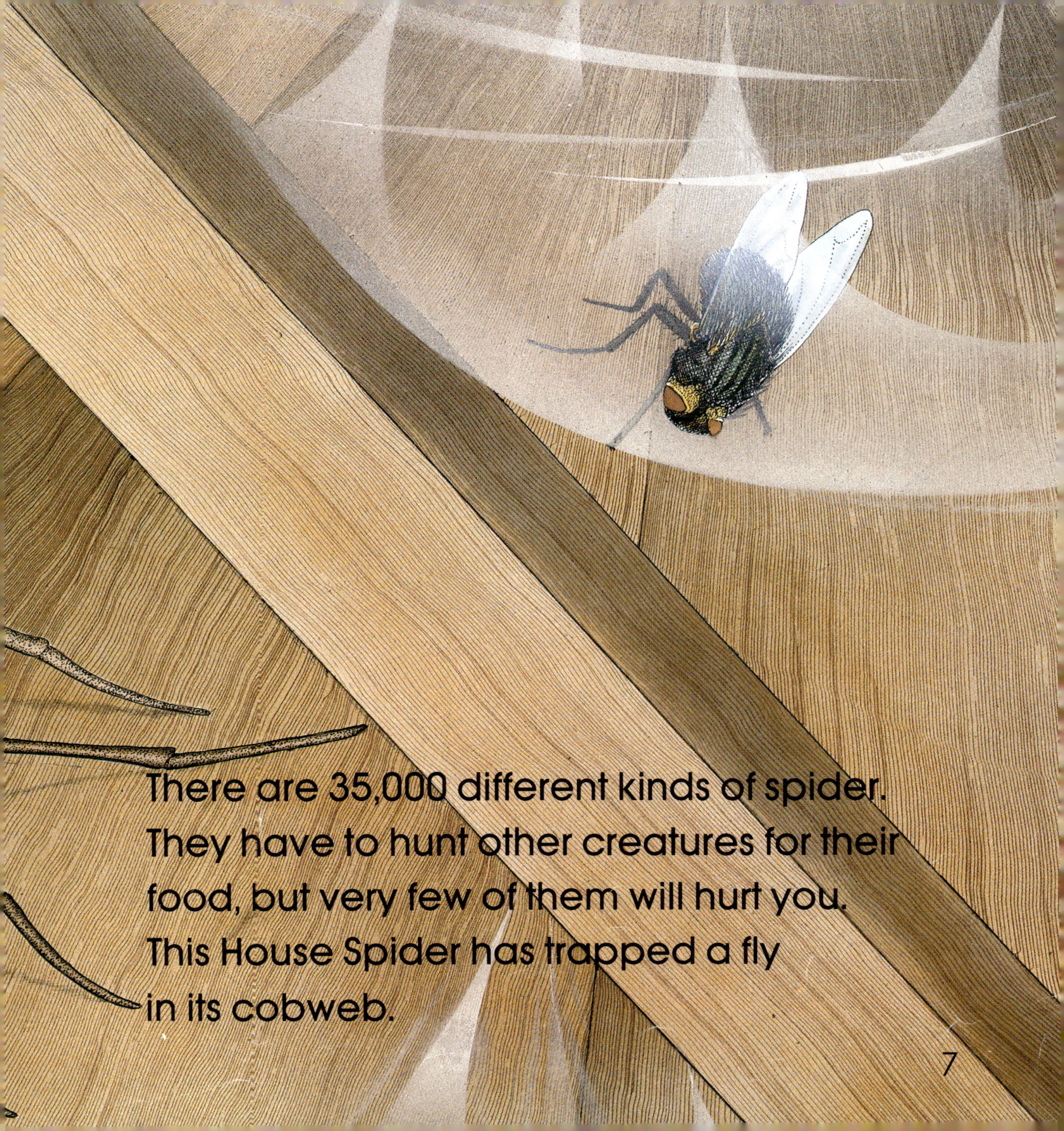

There are 35,000 different kinds of spider. They have to hunt other creatures for their food, but very few of them will hurt you. This House Spider has trapped a fly in its cobweb.

A spider weaves a web from silk which comes from its "spinnerets". They are like six little jets on the underside of its body. The silk is stronger than steel wire of the same thickness.

Size (female): 12-15mm

Spiders' webs are almost invisible, but you can see them on a dewy or frosty morning. Threads of gossamer are left by spiders as they jump or fly off on the breeze.

Different sorts of spiders weave different webs. The Garden Spider always makes its web like this. First it attaches the corner threads to twigs or leaves. Then it makes the “spokes” of the wheel.

It strengthens the centre with a spiral frame. Finally it weaves the sticky main spiral, working inwards from the outside. The spider sits in the middle. It can feel if anything touches the web.

Now the spider waits for an insect to fly into the web and be trapped in the sticky threads. The Hammock Spider can feel the vibrations when an insect drops down into the web.

This spider has injected a poison with its fangs. Now it binds the insect with sticky thread. Spiders eat by sucking out all the juices of their victims.

Male spiders are usually much smaller than the females. This Garden Spider is visiting a female in her web. He taps out a message to let her know who is calling. He doesn't want to be her lunch.

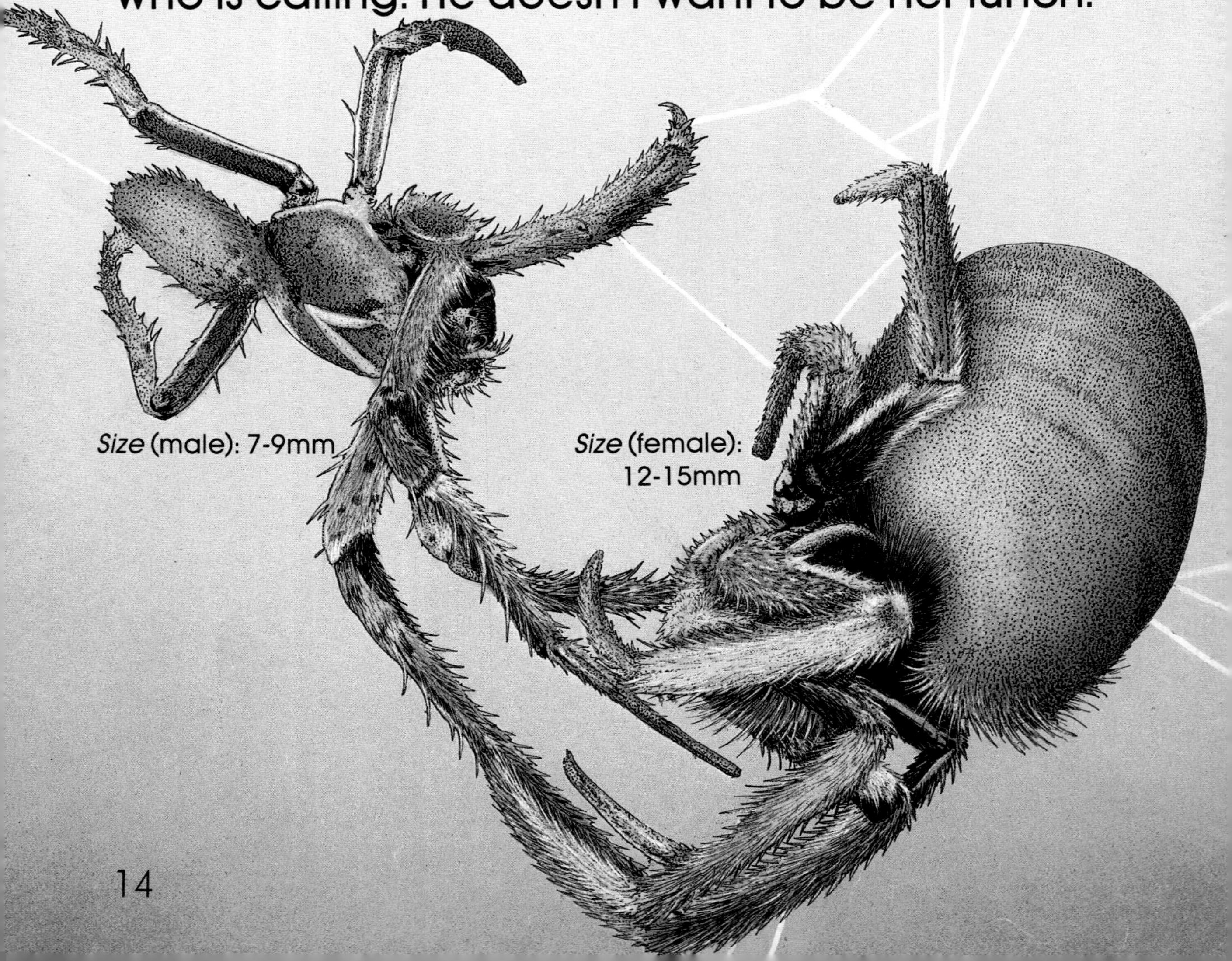

The female Malmignette often eats her mate. She is closely related to the American Black Widow. Both spiders can kill a human with a bite from their poisonous fangs.

Size (female): 16-20mm

All spiders hatch from eggs. A mother spider may lay as few as two eggs or as many as 2,000. She makes a cocoon from silk. This is a Golden Garden Spider's egg-sac.

Wolf spiders have no webs as homes, so they carry their egg-sacs around with them. When the spiderlings hatch they ride around on their mothers' backs. This one has about forty babies.

Wolf spiders don't build webs to trap insects. They chase after them. Wolf spiders can run very fast and they have sharp eyes. You often see them scuttling across the ground.

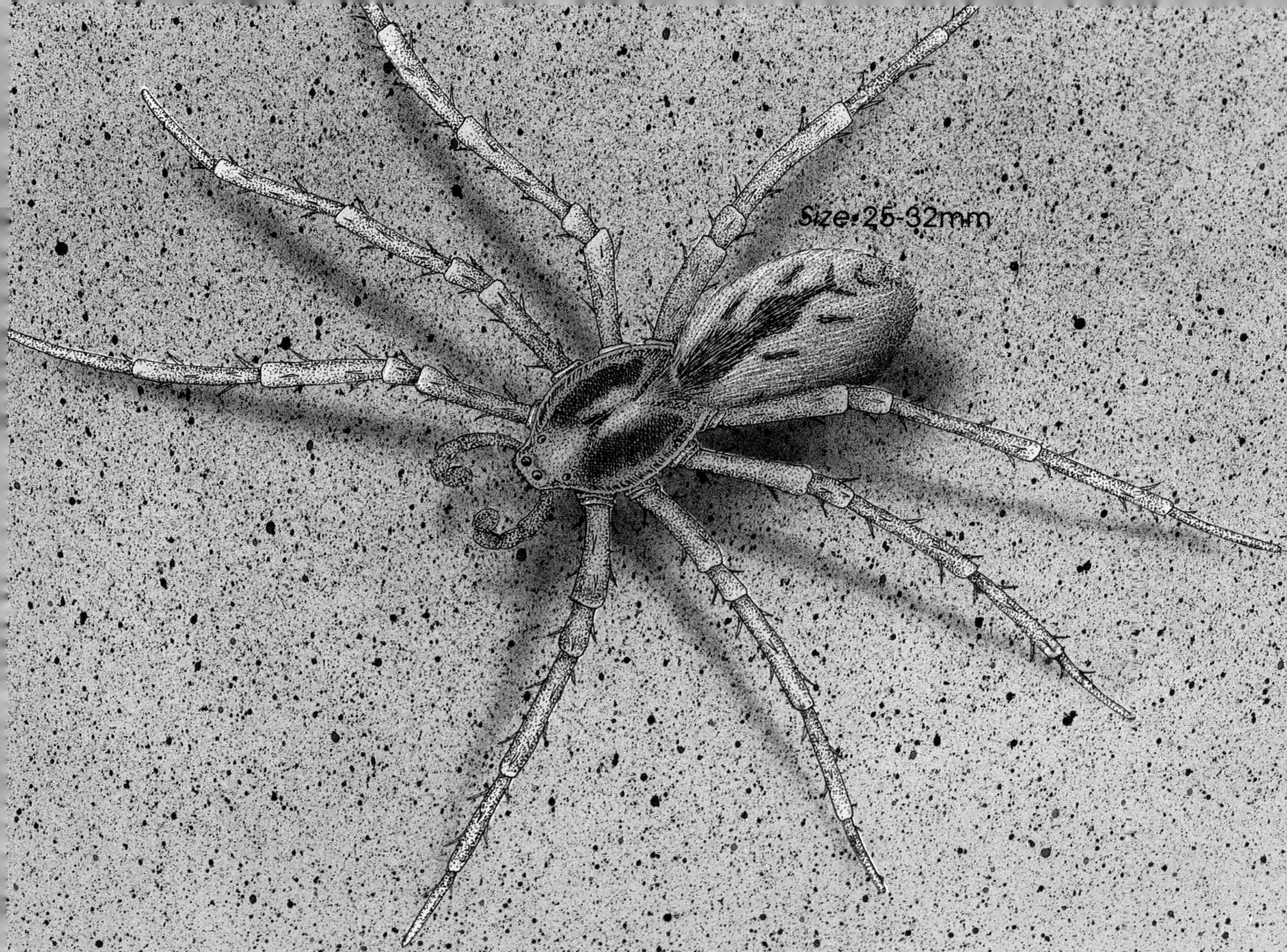

Did you know that a Tarantula looks like this?
Its bite is poisonous, but not deadly.
Like all wolf spiders, the male attracts the female with a special dance.

This Trapdoor Spider comes from America.
Its home is a burrow lined with silk.
The spider lies in wait at the entrance.

The Funnel-web of Australia is another sort of trapdoor spider. It weaves a funnel-shaped web. Australian children know not to touch this spider, as its bite could kill them.

Water Spiders make their homes under water. They carry bubbles of air around with them so they can breathe. Mostly they catch insects. This one is eating a tiny minnow.

Size: 12-14mm

The Water Spider's web is like a diving bell anchored to the water weeds. The female fills it with bubbles of air. She lays her eggs in it and goes to sleep there in the winter.

The little Zebra Spider pounces on insects. It is a jumping spider. It trails a line of silk behind it to save it from falling. Look out for them on a tree stump or a garden wall.

Crab spiders scuttle sideways like crabs. Some of them are brightly coloured, like the flowers they hide in. They can grab butterflies and bees which are hunting for nectar.

Size (female): 6mm

Spiders have many enemies. They are eaten by all sorts of animals, as well as other spiders. This wasp paralyses the spider and lays an egg on it. The maggot feeds on the live spider.

Size: 100-200mm

Although a mother spider may lay hundreds of eggs only one or two will grow up to have babies of their own. One huge pet Bird-eating Spider lived to be twenty years old.

Look back and find

What kind of spider wove this web?

When do spiders weave their webs?
Some spiders build a new web every night.

How do spiders learn to build webs?
They build them by instinct. A baby spider has no trouble building its first web.

How does a spider know it has trapped an insect in its web?

How do spiders eat?
Spiders' mouths are too small to swallow solids. They inject juices which turn the soft parts of the insect to liquid.

Where do Trapdoor Spiders weave their webs?
Inside a long tunnel that they have dug out with their fangs. The "door" is made from soil and silk to fit the opening.

Do you know any other trapdoor spiders?
The Funnel-web is a trapdoor spider, so is the Bird-eating Spider.

What sort of spider is the Tarantula?
This Tarantula is a wolf spider. The Bird-eating Spider is sometimes called a tarantula too.

Why should a dance called the "Tarantella" be connected with the Tarantula?
It was a special dance invented to cure people who had been bitten by a Tarantula.

How big is a Water Spider?

Does the Water Spider trap insects in its web?
No. The Water Spider is a wolf spider that hunts for its prey, but vibrations of the supporting threads of its web tell it that the prey is near by.

How do crab spiders hide themselves?
Different crab spiders look like different leaves and flowers, so they are beautifully camouflaged. Some of them can even change their colour to match their backgrounds.

What kinds of insects do crab spiders eat?

Index